COUNTRY INSIGHTS

CHINA

Julia Waterlow

HODDER
Wayland

an imprint of Hodder Children's Books

COUNTRY INSIGHTS

BRAZIL • CHINA • CZECH REPUBLIC • DENMARK • FRANCE
INDIA • JAPAN • KENYA

For more information on this series and other Hodder Wayland titles, go to www.hodderwayland.co.uk

GUIDE TO THIS BOOK

As well as telling you about the whole of China, this book looks closely at the city of Lanzhou and the village of Shidong.

 This city symbol will appear at the top of the page and information boxes each time the book looks at Lanzhou.

 This rural symbol will appear each time the book looks at Shidong.

Cover photograph: A group of friends look at a laptop in China.

Title page: Loading the bicycle to go home after the weekly market in Rongshui.

Contents page: Taking the waterbuffalo and its calf out to graze.

Series and book editor: Polly Goodman
Series and book designer: Tim Mayer
Production contoller: Caroline Davis
Consultant: Dr Tony Binns, Geography lecturer and tutor of student teachers at the University of Sussex.

First published in 1996 by Wayland Publishers Ltd

Revised and updated in 2006 by Hodder Wayland, an imprint of Hodder Children's Books

British Library Cataloguing in Publication Data
Morrison, Marion
    China. – (Country Insights)
    1. China – Juvenile literature
    I. Title
    951'.059

ISBN 0 7502 4819 X

Typeset by Tim Mayer, England
Printed in China.

Picture acknowledgements:
All photographs except those listed below are by Gordon Clements, of Axiom Photographic Agency. Cover, p29, p31: Eye Ubiquitous (Julia Waterlow); p13, p15, p26, p31: Wayland Picture Library (Julia Waterlow).

Map artwork: page 5: Peter Bull; pages 7 and 8: Hardlines.

Hodder Children's Books
A division of Hodder Headline Limited
338 Euston Road, London NW1 3BH

Contents

寧
咸
邦
萬

The Great Wall of China. Parts of the wall are over 2,000 years old.

Changing China

One of the most famous sights in China is the Great Wall, which stretches 4,000 kilometres across northern China. It was built hundreds of years ago to keep out enemy armies from the north. Deserts, seas and mountains surround China. These barriers, and a mistrust of foreigners, have isolated China from the rest of the world.

China has one of the world's oldest civilizations. In the seventeenth century, however, it fell behind other developing countries. For hundreds of years, China was a land where rich landlords ruled desperately poor people, most of whom were farmers in the countryside. In 1949, a communist government came to power. It made many changes that improved the standard of living for most Chinese. However, the government strictly controlled what people could do or say, and where they could live or work. Few people had any free time or money.

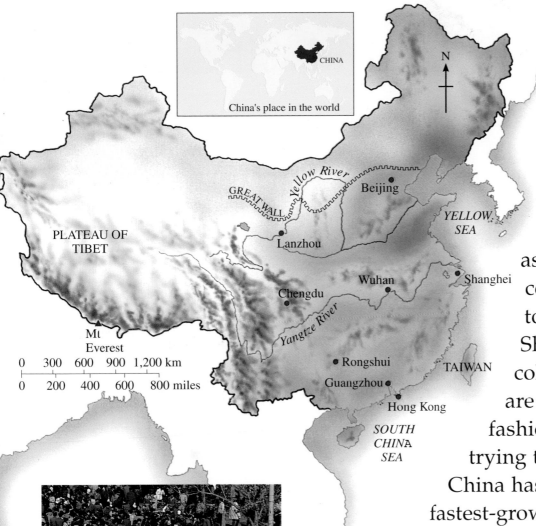

China's place in the world

CHINA

N

Yellow River

GREAT WALL

Beijing

YELLOW SEA

PLATEAU OF TIBET

Lanzhou

Wuhan

Shanghei

Chengdu

Yangtze River

Mt Everest

| 0 | 300 | 600 | 900 | 1,200 km |
| 0 | 200 | 400 | 600 | 800 miles |

Rongshui

TAIWAN

Guangzhou

Hong Kong

SOUTH CHINA SEA

This book takes you to the city of Lanzhou and the village of Shidong, as well as the rest of China. You can find these places on the map.

Now, the Chinese are being allowed more freedom to do as they want and the country is opening up to the outside world. Shops are full and colourful, and clothes are becoming bright and fashionable. People are busy trying to make money and China has one of the world's fastest-growing economies.

Not everyone is better off as a result of these changes. The gap between the rich and poor is getting wider. Although city Chinese may have satellite television and a computer, many people in the countryside still fetch their water from wells every day and struggle to feed themselves and their families.

A busy, crowded market in Lanzhou city.

A VAST LAND	
Total land area:	9.32 million km²
Population:	1.3 billion
Capital city:	Beijing
Highest mountain:	Mt Everest 8,848 m

Lanzhou: Orchid City

Lanzhou (pronounced 'Lan-jo') is the capital city of Gansu, a province in northern China. Although its name means 'orchid city', Lanzhou is a large industrial city with many factories and offices. Shops and restaurants line wide avenues, and taxis and buses sit nose-to-tail on the city streets.

LANZHOU CITY

City area: 13,100 km²
Population: 3.14 million
Race: 92.1 per cent of the population is Han Chinese. The rest belong to minority groups of people.

A view over Lanzhou city and the Yellow River, which runs beside it.

For centuries, Lanzhou was an important city because it was on a great trade route, known as the Silk Road. Merchants used to take beautiful silk cloth made in China westwards on the long journey to Europe. In those days, Lanzhou lay near the borders of China and it was the last major Chinese city travellers saw before they headed out across the deserts to the west.

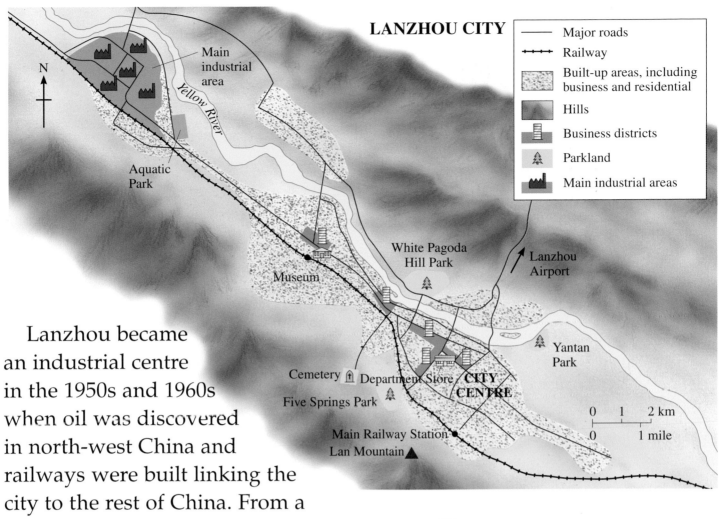

Major roads

+++++ Railway

Built-up areas, including business and residential

Hills

Business districts

Parkland

Main industrial areas

Main industrial area

Yellow River

Aquatic Park

N

Museum

White Pagoda Hill Park

Lanzhou Airport

Yantan Park

Cemetery   Department Store   **CITY CENTRE**

Five Springs Park

Main Railway Station

Lan Mountain

0   1   2 km

0   1 mile

Lanzhou became an industrial centre in the 1950s and 1960s when oil was discovered in north-west China and railways were built linking the city to the rest of China. From a population of about 200,000 in 1949, Lanzhou has grown to over 3 million.

Since the city lies near the edge of what were once China's borders, the people of Lanzhou are not all Chinese. Some are minority people who belong to different races. The largest group are Muslims, although there are also Tibetans and other smaller groups such as the Tuzu, who come from the mountains nearby. These groups have different customs, beliefs and languages from the Chinese, although most also speak Chinese.

Tibetan monks in Lanzhou, wearing their traditional long, red robes.

Shidong: A Scattered Village

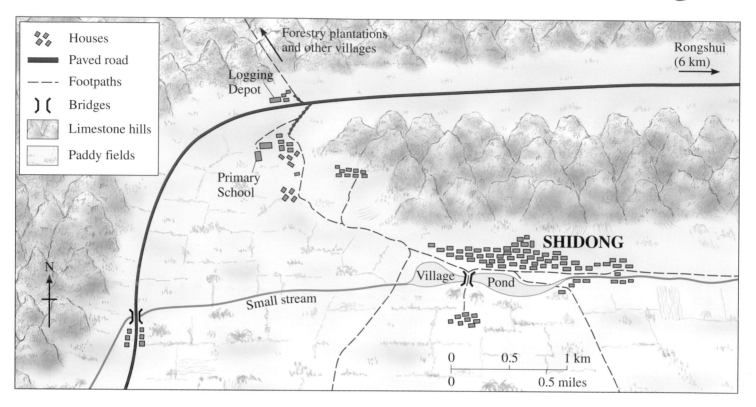

Houses	
Paved road	
Footpaths	
Bridges	
Limestone hills	
Paddy fields	

Forestry plantations and other villages

Rongshui (6 km)

Logging Depot

Primary School

SHIDONG

Village

Pond

Small stream

N

0   0.5   1 km
0   0.5 miles

The village of Shidong nestles at the foot of limestone hills.

The village of Shidong lies in the southern Chinese province of Guangxi, 6 kilometres from the market town of Rongshui. It is one of eleven villages that are scattered around the town. Shidong has a population of 200 people, made up of only about forty families. Nearly all the villagers are farmers.

The villagers of Shidong seldom travel far from their homes, and most never go further than Rongshui. The surrounding roads are rough and buses bump slowly along. Although there is now a narrow road leading to the town, most people take the short cut across the fields. Other than

Rongshui, the nearest large town of Liuzhou lies 100 kilometres away and takes about two hours to get to by bus. Although trains pass through Rongshui twice a day, they are even slower than the buses.

For some families, life in Shidong is not very different from what it would have been hundreds of years ago. In the surrounding hills, people live in very poor conditions working hard on the land to grow enough to eat. Villagers say that their lives are still bitter and harsh.

▲ *A villager carries her produce to the market at Rongshui, 6 kilometres away.*

GETTING AROUND

Few villagers have any means of transport and are used to walking long distances to other villages, the fields and the town. They have to carry everything themselves. Often they balance a wooden pole on their shoulders with baskets slung on each end.

▼ *Bringing the waterbuffaloes home. Waterbuffaloes are used to help plough the fields.*

Landscape and climate

寧咸邦

Most of China's millions of people are crowded into the eastern half of the country because much of western China is either high mountain plateau or, in the far north-west, desert. In these remote regions, the few people who live there keep animals that graze the sparse grass in the cold and bleak mountains, or grow crops in sheltered valleys or well-watered oases.

Eastern China is flatter, and is crossed by two great rivers, the Yellow and the Yangtze, which wind about 6,000 kilometres east to the coast. The valleys of these rivers are the most populated parts of China because they provide a regular supply of water and good, fertile land for farming. The east of China also has more people because the flat land makes it easier to transport goods. People are able to travel on rivers and canals as well as railways and roads. Most of China's large cities are found in the east, and now that trade with the outside world is increasing, those near the coast, such as Shanghai and Guangzhou, are growing fastest.

Southern China's weather is different from northern China. The south is warm and wet all year round so the land is greener. The north has much less rain, and although summers are hot, winters can be freezing cold.

Horses graze below snow-capped mountain peaks in north-west China.

10

CHINA'S LAND USE

Mountains or hills:	65%
Forest:	13%
Crops:	10%
Other (deserts, swamps, urban areas):	12%

During the summer in northern China, everyone lends a hand to bring in the wheat harvest.

Beside the Yellow River

Lanzhou lies on the banks of the Yellow River. There are steep hills all around, so the city weaves like a ribbon along the valley bottom, stretching for nearly 30 kilometres. Not far to the west, the high mountains and deserts of western China begin.

Factories in Lanzhou spread along the banks of the Yellow River.

The Yellow River is famous in China as the birthplace of Chinese civilization, since it was in the Yellow River valley that China's first cities were built, about 3,000 years ago. The river is named after its muddy yellow colour, which is caused by the huge amounts of silt that it carries downstream. This is because the hills around Lanzhou, and a vast region of China to the east, are made of a pale, yellow earth which is very soft. Rain cuts deep ravines into this earth, eroding the soil and washing it into the Yellow River.

Farming around Lanzhou is difficult, partly because it is so hilly. Little grows during the cold winter months and rainfall is very low and unreliable. There can be droughts and then sudden storms which wash away fields, crops and roads.

LANZHOU'S CLIMATE

Average temperatures
  January: −7.2 °C
  July :   21.9 °C
Average annual rainfall: 300 mm

Even so, farmers cut terraces in the hillsides and grow wheat, millet, and tobacco. Wheat, rather than rice, grows best in this cold, dry climate and it is the main food crop and staple diet, as in all of north China. Near the river, where there is more water, vegetables and fruit such as peaches and watermelons grow well in the warm summer months.

▲ *Fields perch above deep gullies cut by rivers in the soft, yellow soil near Lanzhou.*

'**We sometimes have dust storms in Lanzhou that blot out the sun.'**
– Guangu Bai, market trader

◄ *Mr Bai sells melon seeds and peanuts in a market in Lanzhou.*

DUSTY SOIL

Winds blow dust from the dry, desert regions to the north-west of Lanzhou across a huge part of northern China. Over millions of years, this has settled as a thick blanket of fine soil. The land was once covered in trees, but these were cleared by farmers, leaving the soft earth open to erosion by rain and streams. Now, farmers are being advised to plant trees again to hold the soil in place and prevent erosion.

'Meeting Waters'

Shidong is green and lush for most of the year. It is never very cold, but it is often wet – the local people say that you are lucky to get three days' sunshine in a row. A stream flows beside the village and the countryside around is crossed by other streams and rivers. This is how the town of Rongshui, which means 'meeting waters', got its name.

'I usually wear a hat when I go out as it is either raining or the sun is very hot.'
– Xu Meihua, farmer

Although there are hills not far away, the village lies on fairly flat land. In places, steep-sided pinnacles of rock jut up, covered in bushes and trees. The pinnacles are made of a rock called limestone, which has joints and crevices. Rainwater wears away the crevices, often carving out caves and strange shapes in the rock.

Clumps of bamboo grow close to the streams. Their strong stems are used to build rafts and poles. In hills to the west of the village there are forests. But there is little other wild landscape because most of the land is used for farming and trees have been cut down for fuel. With such a large population to feed, the Chinese have to use every bit of land they can.

FOOD FROM THE WILD

Fish in the stream beside Shidong provide an important cheap source of food for the villagers. The village also has a small fish pond where fish are kept and fed scraps of food. People also catch wild creatures such as snakes and freshwater turtles to eat.

◀ *A field of rapeseed in front of limesone pinnacles, which dot the landscape around Shidong. Rapeseed is grown in winter and is used to make oil.*

The warm, wet climate of the village is ideal for growing rice, which is planted in water-filled fields called paddy fields. The paddy fields have low banks around them to keep the water in. When the rice shoots sprout, the village seems to be set in a bright green sea. Farmers are usually able to grow two rice crops a year because it is so warm.

SHIDONG'S CLIMATE

Average temperatures
January:	6.5 °C
July:	27.3 °C

Average annual rainfall: 2,650 mm

A villager plants neat rows of rice seedlings in a paddy field in the summer.

Home life

The Chinese traditionally thought that a large family was a blessing, so people used to have as many children as possible. In the late 1970s, however, the government realized that China's population was growing at an alarming rate. So it told people that in future, they would only be allowed to have one child. They also encouraged young people to get married later.

As a result, many Chinese families are now parents with just one child, although grandparents often live in the home as well. Without brothers and sisters, all the family's attention goes to the single child, who can become quite spoilt.

'We can only have one child, of course. It is the law. Many couples in cities now only want one child. A small family is better in the city.' – Dong Po Wang, Factory manager and father, Beijing.

Mr Wang and his family in Beijing. His wife is wearing a mask because of air pollution in the city.

The Chinese nickname for these single, often spoilt children is 'little emperors'. It is strange to think that many of China's children will grow up not having to use the words 'brother', 'sister', 'uncle' or 'aunt'.

Homes are very different around China. In some of the wilder, more remote areas, such as Tibet and northern China, nomadic herders live in tents instead of houses. Older houses in towns and in mountain areas are sometimes made of wood, but because wood is scarce in most of China, houses are usually built with bricks.

▼ *Most city Chinese live in blocks of flats, like these ones in Lanzhou.*

▼ *This family lives in a tent in north-west China. They are herders and move their home whenever they need to find fresh grazing for their sheep and goats.*

A crowded city

Most people in Lanzhou live in flats because the city is so crowded and there is little space for building. It is the same in all large Chinese cities. A family with parents, one child and grandparents will often have no more than one or two rooms. The luckier ones may have a small kitchen, a toilet and perhaps a shower, but some have to share these with neighbours.

Huasheng's family live in a traditional single-storey house in Lanzhou. They keep their bicycle outside.

In older parts of Lanzhou there are still one or two-storey houses. These are often built round a small courtyard, where families share a tap, a toilet and a communal cooking area. There is also space to hang out washing and grow a few pot plants. Many families in Lanzhou can now afford to buy luxuries like a television, a refrigerator and a washing machine. Few people in the city have cars, but instead, most families have bicycles.

LIVING SPACE

Since Lanzhou is very crowded, flats and homes are very small. People in these homes might have as little as 8 m² per person to live in.

Most people wake up early in the city, usually at about 6 am. After breakfast, the children to go to school and the parents to go to work. Families usually have an early supper together when they come home, and go to bed at about 9 or 10 pm.

Families in Lanzhou eat noodles (made of wheat) every day rather than rice. The noodles are boiled or fried in a large pan called a wok, and everyone eats using bowls and chopsticks. With the noodles they have a little meat and vegetables, and to drink they have tea (without milk). Lanzhou has many street markets where people can buy all kinds of fresh vegetables.

Huasheng's father, Shangjun, stir-fries vegetables in a wok.

'My family has a bicycle. I sit on the crossbar in front of my Dad, and Mum rides on the back.' – Huasheng Li, 8 years old.

A family meal in one of Lanzhou's many street stalls.

Simple homes

It has been difficult to make farmers in Shidong accept that they should only have one child. They see children as necessary to help on the land, especially boys. Because of these traditional views, if the first child is a girl, families are allowed to have a second child.

Many families in the village are very poor and have few possessions. Some people have managed to save enough money to buy a bicycle or a radio, but not many families in the village have a television.

Most houses in the village are made of mud-bricks. Inside, there may be about four rooms with hard earth or stone floors. Families have a few pieces of wooden or bamboo furniture, but no carpets or curtains. It is quite dark inside because the windows are small and the bare electric light is very weak.

Village children eating their lunch outside their house.

LIVING SPACE IN SHIDONG

Although people in Shidong are poorer than people in Lanzhou, they have more space in and around their homes. They might have over 20 m² per person to live in.

Few villagers have water piped to their homes. Instead, they collect drinking water from taps in the village. They wash their clothes in the stream that flows past the village and share outside toilets.

People usually have boiled rice for their meals, often just with some vegetables. Meat costs too much to eat every day and poorer villagers can only treat themselves occasionally to a little pork or fish to go with their rice. Pork comes from the couple of pigs many families keep in their backyard.

▲ *Village children gather firewood for cooking.*

'My mum washes our clothes in the stream near our village. I always help her if I'm not at school.' – Xiaoli, 6 years old (below).

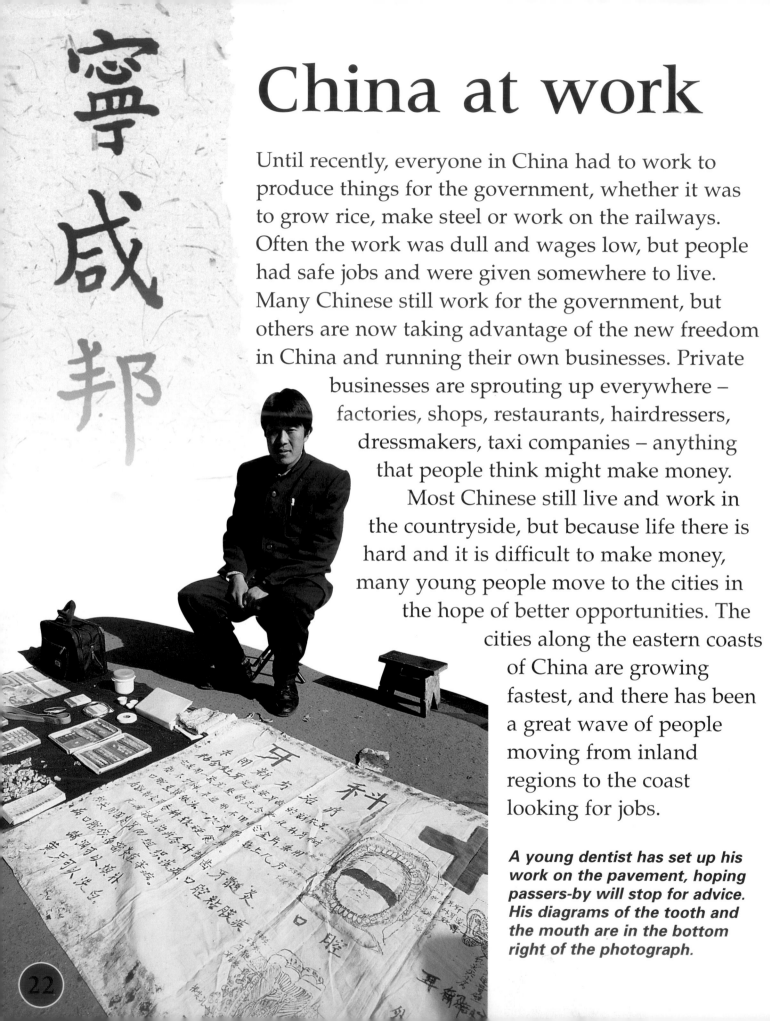

China at work

寧咸邦

Until recently, everyone in China had to work to produce things for the government, whether it was to grow rice, make steel or work on the railways. Often the work was dull and wages low, but people had safe jobs and were given somewhere to live. Many Chinese still work for the government, but others are now taking advantage of the new freedom in China and running their own businesses. Private businesses are sprouting up everywhere – factories, shops, restaurants, hairdressers, dressmakers, taxi companies – anything that people think might make money. Most Chinese still live and work in the countryside, but because life there is hard and it is difficult to make money, many young people move to the cities in the hope of better opportunities. The cities along the eastern coasts of China are growing fastest, and there has been a great wave of people moving from inland regions to the coast looking for jobs.

A young dentist has set up his work on the pavement, hoping passers-by will stop for advice. His diagrams of the tooth and the mouth are in the bottom right of the photograph.

▲ *Many people have started their businesses with market stalls selling clothes and shoes.*

Life in the cities is not always better than the countryside. Unless they know someone who can help, newcomers can find it hard to get a job, and work is often for long hours at low pay. Trying to find somewhere to live is difficult and many end up in crowded dormitories with other workers.

Nearly all women in China work, many doing the same kinds of jobs as men. Until very recently, the Chinese used to work six days a week, but now employers are gradually changing to a five-day week so that people have the weekend free.

WORK IN CHINA	
Type of work	Percentage of workforce
Agriculture	49
Services	29
Industry	22

▼ *These young people from the countryside have arrived in the city without work or anywhere to live.*

Factories and business

Huge oil-processing factories employ thousands of people in Lanzhou. The oil is piped long distances from the deserts west of Lanzhou to the city, where it is made into chemicals, fertilizers and plastics. Other factories make machinery and textiles. They all need good supplies of water, so the factories have been built beside the Yellow River, many in the newer, industrial part of town, west of the centre. Much of the machinery is old and there is little control over safety and pollution.

The government runs many of the factories. Although the pay is not high, the workers are given flats to live in, schooling for their children, medical care and a few have leisure facilities. Company buses take the workers to the factories, while others make their own way by bicycle.

Biking to work in the Lanzhou rush-hour.

'Lanzhou gets very busy in the rush-hour. There are lots of bicycles and buses.' – Sheng Zhiqi, factory manager.

▲ *Lanzhou's huge oil-processing factories pour out smoke and fumes.*

Other people in Lanzhou work in offices, schools, hospitals, restaurants, markets, shops and on the railways and buses – all the usual city jobs. People come from the countryside to find jobs in Lanzhou and many end up as labourers on building sites. As in other Chinese cities, there are new buildings being built everywhere.

Some people in Lanzhou now work for private businesses, not for the government. They can earn more money, but lose benefits such as cheap housing that go with a government job. To get the best of both worlds, in some families one parent keeps their government job and the other works for a private company or runs their own business.

WEALTH IN LANZHOU

People in Chinese cities earned an average of 8475 yuan (about £570) a month in 2003. People in Lanzhou can only afford to spend about half of what people in Shanghai, China's richest city, spend in a year.

This stallholder ▶ *in Lanzhou has done well running his own business selling trainers.*

Working in the fields

Most of the Shidong villagers grow rice. Some times of the year are busier than others, such as at planting and harvest time, when everybody lends a hand to get the work done. Men tend to do work like ploughing and repairing the water channels that feed the paddy fields and women do most of the rice planting. It is hard work because the villagers cannot afford much machinery and have to do many jobs by hand. They use cows or waterbuffaloes to do heavy work like ploughing and some villages share a tractor to transport the produce around.

A buffalo is used to harvest the rice.

As well as rice, the villagers grow maize, sugar cane, sweet potatoes, beans, rape-seed and many different kinds of fruit. Everyone grows vegetables around their houses and families often have a pig or chickens that scavenge for food in the courtyard outside the house or in the village streets. Fields cannot be spared to grow grass for animals, so cows are taken out to graze on field edges or roadsides.

WEALTH IN SHIDONG

People in the Chinese countryside earned an average of 2624 yuan (about £177) a month in 2003, but many still struggle to earn this much in a year. People in Shidong can only afford to spend a third of what people in Lanzhou spend in a year.

VILLAGE TOWNSHIP ENTERPRISES

Many people in the countryside are now working in small industries and businesses set up by villages and towns. These are known in China as 'village township enterprises'.

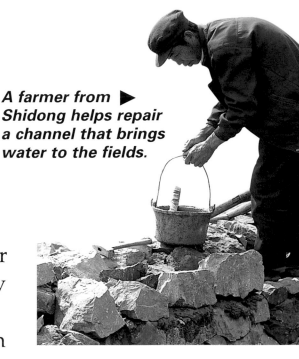

A farmer from ▶ Shidong helps repair a channel that brings water to the fields.

The villagers grow enough food to live off and a little extra to sell. They spend most of their money on food and other basic needs, and rarely buy new clothes.

Some villagers have set up new businesses in the hope of making more money. For example, one group has started a fish farm, while another has set up a brick-making business. Some of the younger people now work in Rongshui for small factories or businesses around the town, such as the cement works and the minibus company.

▼ Villagers have set up a small business raising fish in specially built ponds.

Going to school

Learning has always been thought of highly in China, but education used to be available only to the rich. The majority of people who worked in the countryside never had a chance to read and learn.

When the communist government came to power in 1949, only one person in five could read and write. The government made great improvements, building schools and providing people with basic learning skills. Now all young Chinese spend some time at school, and only about ten per cent of the population cannot read and write properly. There used to be few places available in further education, but the number of people going to college or university after secondary school has more than tripled in the last 15 years.

There is no alphabet in Chinese. Instead, from an early age children learn to write characters. A character represents a word and has its own pronunciation and meaning. Each one has to be learnt by heart, which takes a lot of hard study. Although there are more than 50,000 Chinese characters, most children will learn about 3,000 at primary school.

Chinese children are supposed to have at least nine years' education at school. These children are at a primary school in Beijing.

A science lesson at a secondary school.

SCHOOL IN CHINA	
Starting age:	
Primary	6 or 7 years
Secondary	11 or 12 years
College	16 years
Number of days:	5 days a week
Times:	7 am–5 pm
Lunch:	2 hours
Number of holidays:	Two 5-week holidays a year

Writing, like painting, is thought of as an art, and a brush is used to paint beautiful characters.

Chinese children are mostly well-behaved and very keen students. From an early age they are brought up to be obedient to their parents and teachers, and they know that to do well they must work hard.

This man is writing Chinese ▶ *words, called characters, on a poster with a brush.*

29

School in Lanzhou

There are over 1,600 primary schools in Lanzhou and over 200 secondary schools, as well as thirty colleges of higher education. Most are run by the government and are free, but classes are crowded, with up to fifty students. Very clever or talented children go to 'key' schools, where classes are smaller and equipment and facilities are better than ordinary schools. Quite a few children have extra private lessons that their parents pay for. With only one child to bring up, parents are very keen to make sure their child has the best education possible. Some students go on to vocational secondary schools, where they learn skills to become engineers, electricians or metalworkers. There are not many college places in Lanzhou for further education, so competition is fierce.

'We like playing basketball after school on the school basketball court.' – Daoli, 16 years old.

Basketball is popular at every school in Lanzhou.

Before 8 am, children in Lanzhou will be making their way to school. They either walk to school or their parents take them on the backs of their bicycles. In their satchels they carry their exercise books and a lunchbox with their midday meal. There are even a few children who arrive by car – but their parents are important officials.

◀ *Every morning these children salute the Chinese flag in the school courtyard.*

At most schools in Lanzhou, the day starts with the students doing exercises in the school courtyard. In their lessons they learn eight basic subjects, including Chinese, mathematics, art and music. As they get older, they study science and a foreign language, usually English. They are given plenty of homework to do when they get home.

EDUCATION IN LANZHOU

Over 97 per cent of all young people in Lanzhou can read and write. Almost all children go to primary school and about 80 per cent go on to secondary school.

▼ *Children learning to read at a primary school in Lanzhou.*

School in Shidong

Very small children in Shidong are either looked after by their grandparents or play on the sides of fields while their parents work. When they are six or seven, they go to the nearest primary school, which is in a village 2 kilometres away. The school consists of two buildings, which have just three simple classrooms and only three teachers. There are about 120 village children, aged from about six to thirteen, but they do not all go to school regularly.

This is the nearest school to Shidong, in another village 2 kilometres away. The school has little equipment and few teachers.

The children walk the 2 kilometres to school through the fields and take it in turns to sweep and tidy their classrooms when they arrive. Each student has an exercise book and pencil, but there are few text books so they have to share. One or two posters brighten up the walls of the classrooms, but the school has little else except benches, tables and a blackboard. Outside, there is a courtyard with a basketball net where the children can play at lunchtime or after school.

'At harvest time, our village school sometimes closes and we all help in the fields.' – Quianju, aged 10 (right).

Some parents in Shidong see little point in their children going to school. The children will not use what they have learnt in school to work on the land when they grow up. Most children never finish primary school and only a few go on to secondary school in Rongshui. Even while they are at school, children are often needed to help in the fields. After school and in their spare time, they often have to help by taking the cow out to graze or tend pigs or ducks.

▼ *A villager helps his son with homework.*

China at play

The Chinese used to have very few free days and often worked hard for seven days a week with no holidays. New laws now allow a two day weekend and holiday weeks during the Chinese New Year and in May and October, when people like to visit friends and family.

Now that more families can afford televisions, many people spend hours glued to their sets. Otherwise they like to be outside because, particularly in the cities, their homes are so small. No one has their own garden in cities and towns, so parks are often crowded. Here people exercise, stroll, play card games or sit and chat. Often there are amusements such as boating lakes, magicians or singers, and places to have a simple snack or drink. Another favourite way of passing the time is to visit a local sight, such as a nearby hill or an old temple.

In cities, many people exercise early in the morning in a park before work.

Although there is traditional Chinese music and opera, many young people now like to listen to pop music, go to discos and sing karaoke. In cities, they are becoming very fashion-conscious and like to spend their spare money on buying clothes, going to the cinema and going out with friends.

▲ Letting off fireworks and lion dancing at Chinese New Year.

The Chinese enjoy sports of all kinds, but they mostly play those that do not need expensive equipment. Volleyball, table tennis, badminton, gymnastics and athletics are especially popular.

The main public holiday in China is the Chinese New Year festival, which falls in either January or February. It is a time when the family gets together, eating and drinking and visiting relatives, and people let off fireworks in the street. Minority people in China have their own special religious festivals, often with singing and dancing.

MAJOR FESTIVALS IN CHINA

The dates of China's festivals vary every year because they are based on the lunar (moon) calendar.

Chinese New Year	January or February
Qing Ming	April
Dragon Boat	July
Moon Festival	October
Public Holidays	
May Day (1 May)	
Children's Day (1 June)	
National Day (1 October)	

◄ Boards outside the cinema show what films are being shown.

Leisure in Lanzhou

Early in the morning, before work, people flock to the banks of the Yellow River in Lanzhou to exercise and dance to recorded music. In other parks and open spaces around the city, others practise *tai chi*, a kind of slow exercise the Chinese believe helps both body and mind.

Younger people play sports at school, and those who show real promise may get special coaching and be able to join a local team. In the evening, after school and homework, if they are not watching television, children go out to play with friends on the streets near their houses.

Sundays are crowded and busy as people go out to relax and enjoy themselves. The popular White Pagoda Hill Park and Five Springs Park wind up the hillsides on both sides of the city.

Playing cards in a park in Lanzhou.

'Chinese TV programmes are often boring and dull. Foreign ones are much more interesting and exciting.' – Huasheng Li, 8 years old (right).

In teahouses on the slopes, people sit quietly sipping tea and playing games such as chess, *mahjong* and cards. Some families take the chairlift to the top of Lan mountain and then wander down pathways admiring the view, having their photographs taken and stopping at drinks stalls on the way.

In the city centre, people stroll around the shops and markets. Not everyone can afford to buy, but they like to look. For a special treat they sometimes stop to enjoy a cheap and tasty bowl of dumplings in Xinan Street.

◄ *Many older men in Lanzhou like to keep songbirds as pets.*

Quiet pastimes

The pace of life in Shidong is very slow and people do not live according to a clock like they do in the cities. There is no regular spare time, except schoolchildren have evenings, weekends and school holidays free. Leisure time depends on the time of year and whether everyone is busy working in the fields.

The villagers do not have money to buy many toys so they make their own, such as kites constructed out of paper and sticks. On hot, summer days, many children join the waterbuffaloes, swimming and splashing in the rivers and streams nearby.

When there is no work to do in the fields, the villagers are busy with other jobs, like washing their clothes or sewing. Often they sit outside their houses talking with neighbours and watching the world go by. The men sometimes share a drink and play a game of cards.

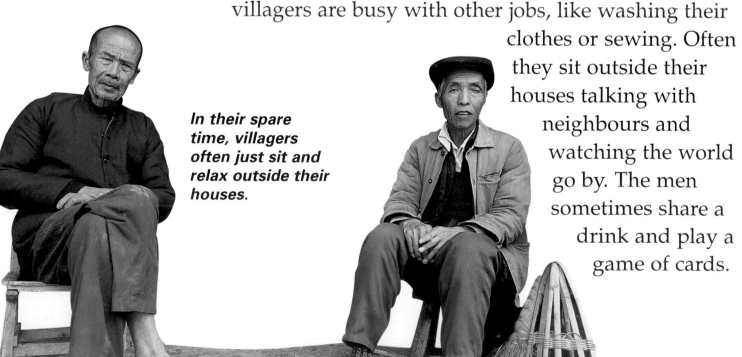

In their spare time, villagers often just sit and relax outside their houses.

▲ *Chickens are bought and sold at the market in Rongshui.*

On Saturdays, it is market day in Rongshui. The villagers travel into town, bringing their vegetables, pigs and chickens to sell. People meet, chat and wander round the shops and stalls. Occasionally they may go and visit the temples at Shouxing Park near Rongshui and pray for good luck, good health, or that they will become richer.

The only time the villagers have a real holiday is at festival times, like the New Year and Moon festivals. At these times the villagers hang out lanterns and prepare special food, such as sweet, sticky rice and delicious moon cakes.

'We play in the fields or in the street when our parents haven't got any jobs for us to do.' – Wenbin, 9 years old (below right).

Facing the future

China has managed to slow its population growth since the government brought in its 'one-child' birth-control policy. If this policy continues to be successful, the Chinese population is expected to start dropping around the year 2030. However, this would cause an ageing population and a weakening workforce, so this strict policy may well be relaxed and the population could reach as many as 1.6 billion by the year 2050.

The extra people will all need water, food, houses and jobs, but China's resources are already stretched. Land in eastern China is crowded and all the best farming land is being used. There are power and water shortages in some cities, roads and railways are jammed with traffic, rivers and air are polluted, and forests are being cut down. Adding to these problems is the need for more raw materials, power and transport to supply China's growing industries and businesses.

KONGZHI REKOUZENGZHANG JIANSHEWENMINGGUOJIA

控制人口增长建设文明国家

常南街办事处宣

This poster encourages people to have only one child, to control China's population.

40

USAGE OF NEW TECHNOLOGY IN CHINA

Since 1978, the Chinese government has been encouraging new businesses and industries to grow to improve the economy. It has been very important for China to use the latest technology in order to communicate well and become an important part of trade throughout the world. While the communist government has strict rules about what people are allowed to read, write and even talk about, it is sometimes hard to apply these rules to new technology such as mobile phones and the Internet. As a result there has been a huge rise in the use of this technology. About 16% of people have mobile phones, 28% have personal computers, and 46% are now Internet users.

In China's big cities, some people have mobile telephones. In the countryside, many do not even have a water tap.

The Chinese are working on thousands of new projects to provide for the future. These include blocks of flats, factories, roads, railways and power stations. The massive hydroelectric scheme that is currently being built on the Yangtze River will be the largest in the world.

Even though China is going to find it difficult to meet all its needs, the future for many young Chinese is better than in the past. They are better educated, richer and there are more chances to find interesting jobs and do well. However, there are more opportunities for people in the cities than for those in the countryside.

Supplying the city

Lanzhou's large population and many industries need a great deal of water and power, and changing lifestyles add to these needs. Many people in Lanzhou are getting richer, and are able to afford items such as washing machines and televisions, which require even more water and electricity. The city will have to meet these demands if it is going to survive in the future.

Lanzhou depends on the Yellow River for water because rainfall in the area is so low. As well as being used by houses and factories, river water is taken by farmers to irrigate their crops. At certain times of the year, the big Liujia reservoir, upstream of Lanzhou is beginning to fall to very low levels.

Coal, which is the main source of fuel used to make electricity, has to be brought from hundreds of kilometres away by train. However, the railway

'There used to be eighteen different kinds of fish in the Yellow River in Lanzhou, but eight are now extinct.' – Huang Wei, retired teacher.

The Liujia reservoir and hydroelectric power station near Lanzhou, where water power is used to make electricity.

▲ *Lanzhou's factories are polluting both air and water in the city.*

system in China is so overcrowded that Lanzhou is sometimes short of coal. The city has one big advantage compared with other Chinese cities for producing power: it lies close to high mountains with plenty of fast-flowing water. Several hydroelectric schemes have been built which may help provide the city with power in the future.

Lanzhou's industries are struggling to compete with more modern industries in richer parts of China and have little spare money to spend on controlling pollution. In parts of the city, the air is filled with evil-smelling chemical fumes and the Yellow River is filled with household waste and chemical waste from the factories. No one would now dare drink from its waters.

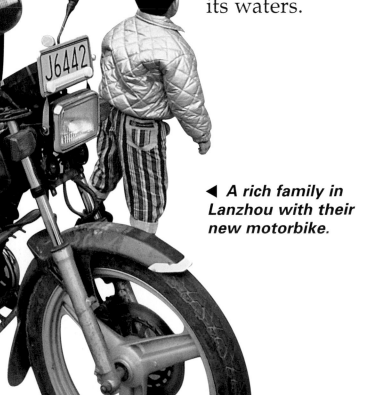

◀ *A rich family in Lanzhou with their new motorbike.*

Changing landscape

This farmer is selling sugar cane. He makes more money selling this crop than rice.

Villages like Shidong are important to China's future. Together, they must produce enough food to feed the enormous population, especially basic foods such as rice and wheat. The village farmers use all the land they possibly can and it would be difficult for them to increase the amount of rice grown. The area of land used for growing rice is actually getting smaller. Fields once used for rice are now being used to grow other crops which make more money, particularly sugar cane and fruit, and farmland is lost as new roads are built and the villages in the area grow.

The villagers, like most rural Chinese, do not see the point of preserving wild countryside or wildlife, so these are fast disappearing. The land is needed to grow crops and many wild plants and animals are used for medicines or are eaten as food. The forests in the mountains to the west of the village are gradually being cut down because wood is needed for fuel and building.

LOSS OF AGRICULTURAL LAND

To become a more modern country, China is encouraging some of its agricultural workers to seek city jobs in industry or services, and agricultural land has been lost to the dramatic expansion of cities in China over the past twenty years. This has made some people worry that China might not be able to make enough food for its huge population in the future, but the government is making plans to ensure that this does not become a problem.

▲ Nearly all the villagers in Shidong grow vegetables and sell them at the market in Rongshui.

▼ A young village girl takes care of her younger sister. As she gets older, this girl will probably have to work in the fields or leave Shidong to find a job in a city.

For the people of Shidong, their most important concern is to get the crops sown, harvested and taken to market. Although villagers are interested in the changes taking place in China, and some hope new village business will bring wealth, most feel it is unlikely there will be much difference to their lives in the near future.

45

Glossary

Civilization A country or state with a high level of art, customs and law.

Communist A follower of the political idea that everything should be owned and controlled by the community and shared between the people.

Droughts Long periods without any rain.

Dumplings Cases of flour containing pieces of meat and vegetables, which are then boiled or fried.

Eroding The wearing away of land and soil by the action of water and wind.

Fertile land Land where crops and other plants grow well.

Fertilizers Substances (usually animal manure or chemicals) put on the land to help crops grow.

Fuel A substance that is burnt to provide heat for cooking or warmth, or to produce power to drive machinery.

Hydroelectric A way of making electricity by using the power of falling water.

Irrigate To supply water to land.

Isolated Cut off from the outside world.

Mahjong A Chinese game which uses small tiles with characters, pictures and numbers on them. Four people sit round a table to play.

Millet A kind of grain grown for food.

Minority A group of people that is different in some way from a larger group of which it is part.

Muslims People who follow the religion founded by the Prophet Mohammed.

Nomadic A way of life that involves moving around rather than living in a fixed place.

Noodles A food made from wheat flour, rather like spaghetti.

Oases Places in the middle of a desert where there is water.

Plateau A large area of high and fairly flat land.

Reservoir An artificial lake where water is stored.

Rape-seed A plant with yellow flowers grown as a crop. The seeds are used to make oil.

Rural In, or belonging to, the countryside.

Silt Very fine particles of mud and soil carried by a river.

Service industries Industries, such as tourism and banking, that do not make goods but supply people with services they need.

Staple diet The main or most important food that someone eats.

Terraces Areas on the side of a slope or hill where farmers have flattened the land so that they can grow crops more easily.

Vocational To do with preparation for a trade or profession.

Further information

Books to read

A River Journey: The Yangtze by Rob Bowden (Hodder Wayland, 2005)

Economically Developing Countries: China by Julia Waterlow (Hodder Wayland, 2001)

China: The New Super Power? by Ewan McLeish and Antony Mason (Franklin Watts, 2005)

Continents of the World: Asia by Rob Bowden (Hodder Wayland, 2005)

Country Files: China by Mike March (Franklin Watts, 2003)

The Changing Face Of: China by Stephen Keeler (Hodder Wayland, 2002)

We Come From: China by Julia Waterlow (Hodder Wayland, 2002)

World In Focus: China by Ali Brownlie Bojang (Hodder Wayland, 2002)

Useful addresses

The Great Britain-China Centre, 15 Belgrave Square, London SW1X 8PS Tel: 020 7235 6696 has a good library with information about all aspects of China, as well as audio and visual information.

Cultural Section, Chinese Embassy, 11 West Heath Road, London NW3 5PA Tel: 020 7794 7595

Sources

The statistics in this book are from the following sources:

Statistical Yearbook of China (China Statistical Publishing House)

BOCOG (en.Beijing-2008.org)

CIA World Factbook (www.cia.gov/cia/publications/factbook/)

National Bureau of Statistics of China (www.stats.gov.cn/english/)

United Nations Population Division (www.un.org/esa/population/unpop.htm)

World Bank (www.worldbank.org)

The website addresses (URLs) included in this book were valid at the time of going to press. However, because of the nature of the Internet, it is possible that some addresses may have changed, or sites may have changed or closed down since publication. While the authors and publisher regret any inconvenience this may cause readers, no responsibility for any such changes can be accepted by either the authors or the publisher.

Index

Page numbers in **bold** refer to photographs.